D1710278

KANSAS
JAYHAWKS

BY DREW SILVERMAN

Published by ABDO Publishing Company, PO Box 398166, Minneapolis, MN 55439. Copyright © 2012 by Abdo Consulting Group, Inc. International copyrights reserved in all countries. No part of this book may be reproduced in any form without written permission from the publisher. SportsZone™ is a trademark and logo of ABDO Publishing Company.

Printed in the United States of America,
North Mankato, Minnesota
102011
012012

Editor: Chrös McDougall
Copy Editor: Anna Comstock
Series design and cover production: Craig Hinton
Interior production: Kelsey Oseid

Photo Credits: Orlin Wagner/AP Images, cover, 38, 42 (bottom right), 44; Chuck Burton/AP Images, 1; Mark Humphrey/AP Images, 4, 43 (bottom); Brett Wilhelm/NCAA Photos/AP Images, 7; Ryan McKee/ NCAA Photos/AP Images, 8; Matt York/AP Images, 11; AP Images, 12, 18, 29, 42 (top), 43 (top right); WPS/AP Images, 14, 20; Collegiate Images/Getty Images, 17, 43 (top left); William P. Straeter/AP Images, 23; Charlie Neibergall/AP Images, 24, 41; Ed Reinke/AP Images, 26, 36, 42 (bottom left); Dave Martin/ AP Images, 30; Susan Ragan/AP Images, 33; Bob Child/AP Images, 34

Design elements: Matthew Brown/iStockphoto

Library of Congress Cataloging-in-Publication Data
Silverman, Drew, 1982-
  Kansas Jayhawks / by Drew Silverman.
    p. cm. -- (Inside college basketball)
  Includes index.
  ISBN 978-1-61783-283-3
  1. Kansas Jayhawks (Basketball team)--History--Juvenile literature. 2. University of Kansas--Basketball- -History--Juvenile literature. I. Title.
  GV885.43.U52S57 2012
  796.323'630978165--dc23

                    2011040001

TABLE OF CONTENTS

Kansas guard Mario Chalmers launches
a three-pointer to take the 2008 NCAA
championship game into overtime.

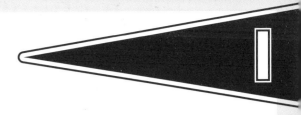

SUPER MARIO

THE BASKETBALL LEFT MARIO CHALMERS'S HANDS. TO FANS OF THE UNIVERSITY OF KANSAS JAYHAWKS, IT SEEMED TO HANG IN THE AIR FOREVER. IN REALITY, IT WAS ONLY A COUPLE OF SECONDS. THEN THE BALL WENT IN THE BASKET. *SWISH*.

Chalmers's three-pointer came in the nick of time. It went through the hoop with 2.1 seconds remaining in the 2008 national championship game. The three points tied the Jayhawks 63–63 with the Memphis Tigers. Kansas went on to beat Memphis in overtime, 75–68. The Jayhawks were champions of the 2008 National Collegiate Athletic Association (NCAA) Tournament.

Chalmers was the hero. Shortly after the game, Jayhawks coach Bill Self said, "It'll probably be the biggest shot ever made in Kansas history." Senior guard Rodrick Stewart took it a step further. "That has to be one of the biggest shots in basketball history," Stewart said.

GOING PRO

Five players from Kansas' 2007–08 national championship team were selected in the 2008 National Basketball Association (NBA) Draft. Brandon Rush (Portland Trail Blazers) and Darrell Arthur (New Orleans Hornets) were first-round picks. Mario Chalmers (Minnesota Timberwolves), Darnell Jackson (Miami Heat), and Sasha Kaun (Seattle SuperSonics) were second-round picks. One additional member of the national championship team, Cole Aldrich, was chosen in the 2010 NBA Draft. He was a first-round pick of the Hornets.

Chalmers, a junior point guard, was named Most Outstanding Player of the Final Four. He finished the championship game with 18 points, four steals, three rebounds, and three assists.

Chalmers had plenty of help from his teammates. In the win over Memphis, sophomore forward Darrell Arthur led Kansas with 20 points and 10 rebounds. Brandon Rush, a junior swingman, added 12 points. And sophomore point guard Sherron Collins had 11 points with six assists.

The 2008 national championship was the Jayhawks' third. The school's other NCAA championships came in 1952 and 1988. For one of the most successful programs in college basketball history, the third title did not come easily.

Chalmers and Rush were freshmen in 2006. The Jayhawks entered the NCAA Tournament that year as a number-four seed. But the thirteenth-seeded Bradley Braves upset the Jayhawks in the first round. That marked the second straight season in which the Jayhawks had suffered a major upset in the tournament's opening round.

The fourteenth-seeded Bucknell Bison had beaten the third-seeded Jayhawks in the first round of the 2005 tournament.

Kansas broke the streak in the 2007 tournament. This time the Jayhawks were a number-one seed. Kansas won its first three games to advance to the Elite Eight. Only the second-seeded University of California, Los Angeles (UCLA) Bruins stood between the Jayhawks and the Final Four. But UCLA won that game 68–55.

As it turned out, the painful NCAA Tournament losses helped make Kansas stronger. The Jayhawks opened the 2007–08 season with 20

consecutive wins. They lost three of their next seven games after that. But the Jayhawks did not lose again that season.

Kansas ended the regular season with four straight wins. Among them was a 109–51 victory against the Texas Tech Red Raiders. The Jayhawks finished with a 13–3 record in Big 12 Conference games. That was enough to earn them their fourth straight regular-season conference title.

The Jayhawks also played well in the Big 12 Conference Tournament. They advanced to the final against the Texas Longhorns. Chalmers gave a preview of what was to come in the NCAA Tournament. He scored 30 points in the win over Texas. It was a new career high for Chalmers. He made 10 of 15 shots, including eight of 12 three-pointers, against the Longhorns.

Kansas entered the 2008 NCAA Tournament as one of the four number-one seeds. And the team played like one of the top four teams in the country. The Jayhawks won their first three games to return to the Elite Eight. This time, a small school called Davidson stood between Kansas and the Final Four. Shooting guard Stephen Curry led the Davidson Wildcats. He had become the breakout star of the tournament.

Curry scored 25 points against Kansas. But he made just nine of 25 shots. On the other hand, Chalmers and senior center Sasha Kaun led the Jayhawks with 13 points apiece. They combined to make 11 of 16 shots. Kansas beat Davidson 59–57 to advance to the Final Four.

The North Carolina Tar Heels awaited the Jayhawks in the Final Four. North Carolina had a star player of its own. Junior forward Tyler Hansbrough was the Naismith College Player of the Year for the 2007–08 season. The award goes to the best player in the country. It was named after Dr. James Naismith. He invented basketball and later became the first coach at Kansas in 1898.

Hansbrough scored 17 points and grabbed nine rebounds against the Jayhawks. But again, Kansas proved to be a better team. The Jayhawks got off to a great start. They led 40–12 at one point late in the first half.

SUPER MARIO

KEYS TO VICTORY

Free-throw shooting and rebounding were two of the biggest keys to Kansas defeating the Memphis Tigers in the NCAA Tournament championship game. The Jayhawks made 14 of 15 foul shots. Meanwhile, the Tigers made just 12 of 19. And Kansas finished with 39 rebounds, compared with only 28 for Memphis.

The Jayhawks went on to win 84–66 to advance to the national championship game. It was their first time in the championship game since 2003.

The Jayhawks faced yet another superstar in the NCAA title game. Memphis freshman point guard Derrick Rose was a third-team All-American. Later that year, the Chicago Bulls selected Rose with the first pick in the National Basketball Association (NBA) Draft. Memphis also had a junior swingman named Chris Douglas-Roberts. He was a first-team All-American in 2007–08.

Kansas, meanwhile, did not have any All-Americans that season. It also did not have any players who would become top 10 picks in the NBA Draft. What the Jayhawks had was a well-balanced team that knew how to win basketball games.

This one took a late rally, though. The Jayhawks were losing by nine with 2:12 left in the second half. Baskets by Arthur and Collins got Kansas a little bit closer. Meanwhile, Memphis stars Rose and Douglas-Roberts missed some key free-throw attempts.

The Jayhawks celebrate with the 2008 NCAA championship trophy after defeating the Memphis Tigers 75–68 in overtime.

Chalmers then made the once-in-a-lifetime shot. Kansas dominated in overtime, and the rest was history. "As soon as it left my hand, it felt good," Chalmers said. "I knew it was going in. I just waited for it to hit the net." For Chalmers and his teammates, it was well worth the wait.

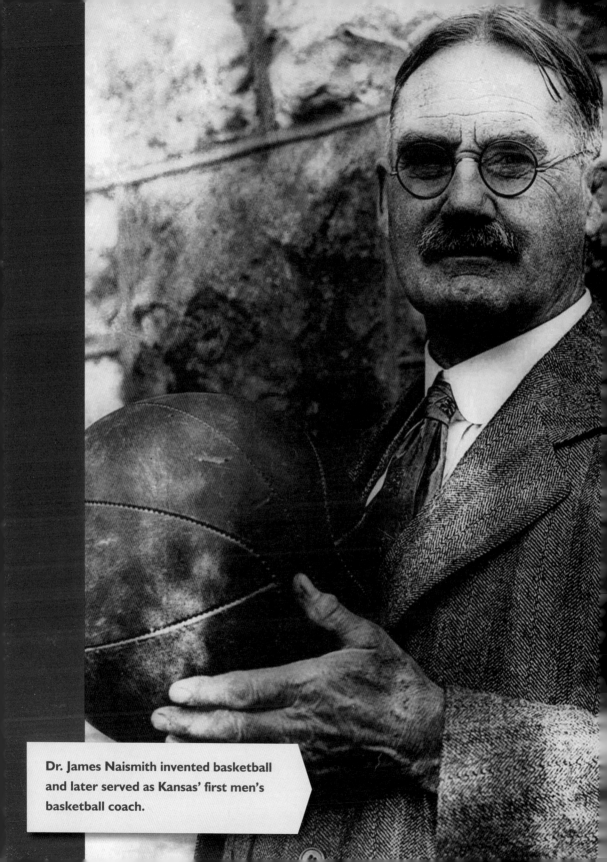

Dr. James Naismith invented basketball and later served as Kansas' first men's basketball coach.

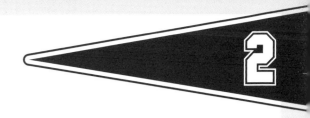

BACK TO BASICS

THE EARLY YEARS OF KANSAS JAYHAWKS BASKETBALL INCLUDE SOME OF THE MOST FAMOUS NAMES IN THE HISTORY OF THE SPORT. RIGHT AT THE TOP OF THAT LIST IS DR. JAMES NAISMITH. HE CREATED THE SPORT OF BASKETBALL IN 1891 WHILE WORKING AS A PHYSICAL EDUCATION INSTRUCTOR IN SPRINGFIELD, MASSACHUSETTS.

Naismith joined the University of Kansas as a professor in 1898. He also became the school's first basketball coach that year. However, Naismith is actually the only coach in Jayhawks history to lose more games than he won. He coached the team for nine seasons. The Jayhawks' record during that time was just 55–60.

Naismith was known as the "Father of Basketball." The next Kansas coach was known as the "Father of Basketball Coaching." That was Forrest "Phog" Allen. He played for Naismith at Kansas and later coached the Jayhawks for 39 seasons. Allen coached the team in 1907–08 and 1908–09

before leaving to study medicine. He returned to Kansas in 1919 and
coached the team through the 1955–56 season.

Allen's Kansas teams won 24 conference championships. The
Jayhawks also won the 1952 NCAA Tournament title under Allen. The
Helms Athletic Foundation retroactively determined college basketball
champions before the NCAA Tournament began in 1939. It decided
Allen's teams from 1922 and 1923 were national champions as well.

Allen had many great players on his Jayhawks teams. Five players
from the 1920s had such outstanding careers at Kansas that the school
later retired their jerseys. Those players were Tus Ackerman, Charlie T.
Black, Paul Endacott, Gale Gordon, and Al Peterson.

According to Allen, Endacott was "the greatest player I have ever coached." The Helms Foundation named Endacott the 1923 National Player of the Year. As team captain that year, Endacott led the Jayhawks to a 17–1 record. That included a 16–0 mark in the Missouri Valley Conference. It was the first undefeated season in the history of the league. Endacott was a two-time All-American for the Jayhawks who was known for his tough defense. In 1972, Endacott was elected to the Naismith Basketball Hall of Fame.

The Jayhawks had two players during the 1930s who stood above the rest. Guard Fred Pralle was Kansas' first consensus All-American. He led Kansas to the Big Six Conference championship in all three of his seasons at the school, from 1935 to 1938. Shortly after Pralle graduated, forward Howard Engleman became the Jayhawks' next star. Engleman was the second Kansas player to be named a consensus All-American. He guided the team to a pair of Big Six championships. He also led Kansas to the 1940 national championship game. However, the Indiana Hoosiers beat the Jayhawks.

Forward Charlie B. Black and guard Ray Evans stood out for the Jayhawks during the 1940s. Both players starred in 1941–42 and 1942–43.

WILLIAM HAMILTON

William Hamilton coached Kansas from 1909 until 1919. During Hamilton's 10 seasons, the Jayhawks won five conference championships, including three in a row between 1910 and 1912. His teams had three All-Americans. They were forward Tommy Johnson in 1909, forward Ralph "Lefty" Sproull in 1915, and guard/forward A. C. "Dutch" Lonborg in 1919.

DEAN SMITH

Junior guard Dean Smith did not see much playing time during Kansas' 1951–52 championship season. He averaged only 1.5 points per game that season. When Smith graduated in 1953, he became an assistant coach under Phog Allen at Kansas. That began a coaching career in which Smith won two national championships as head coach of the North Carolina Tar Heels. When Smith retired in 1997, he had 879 career wins. That was more than any other coach in college basketball history. His wins record stood until 2007, when Bob Knight surpassed him.

Then they starred again in 1946–47 and 1947–48. In between, they each served in the US military during World War II.

Charlie B. Black is the only four-time All-American in the history of Kansas basketball. He was nicknamed "The Hawk" for his tough defense at the forward position. He also was the first player in Jayhawks history to score at least 1,000 points in his career. Evans was an All-American guard on the basketball court. He was also an All-American defensive back for the Kansas football team.

A senior center named Clyde Lovellette led the Jayhawks to their first NCAA Tournament championship in 1952. That season, Lovellette became the only player in NCAA history to lead the nation in points per game and also win the championship in the same season. Lovellette scored 33 points and grabbed 17 rebounds in the 1952 championship game. It was an 80–63 victory against St. John's. Kansas led the entire game and finished the season with a 28–3 record. After college, Lovellette went on to a great NBA career and was elected to the Naismith Basketball Hall of Fame in 1988.

The 1952 Kansas Jayhawks went 28–3 on their way to the school's first national championship.

"The days I spent in Lawrence [Kansas] were just super," Lovellette said during his Hall of Fame induction speech. "I will love Kansas and Lawrence for the rest of my life."

Allen coached Kansas for four more seasons after winning the 1952 NCAA Tournament. His team returned to the NCAA title game in 1953. But the Jayhawks came up just short in that game, losing to Indiana 69–68. Forward Jerry Alberts missed a shot at the buzzer that would have given Kansas its second straight championship.

Allen retired in 1956. He was 70 years old at the time. That was the mandatory retirement age in the state of Kansas. Unfortunately for Allen, that meant he never got a chance to coach the man who changed the face of basketball—both in college and the pros— forever.

Kansas' Wilt Chamberlain grabs a rebound against Oklahoma State during the 1956 Big Seven Tournament.

A NEW GENERATION

KANSAS LOST A LEGEND IN 1956 WITH THE RETIREMENT OF COACH PHOG ALLEN. HOWEVER, THE KANSAS BASKETBALL PROGRAM DID NOT HAVE TO WAIT LONG FOR THE ARRIVAL OF ANOTHER LEGENDARY FIGURE. WILT CHAMBERLAIN JOINED THE JAYHAWKS' VARSITY TEAM FOR THE 1956–57 SEASON. HE WAS A 7-FOOT-1 CENTER WITH MASSIVE SIZE AND TREMENDOUS ABILITY.

Chamberlain went on to become one of the greatest college basketball players of all time. In fact, he went on to become one of the greatest basketball players ever—on any level. His dominance caused both the NCAA and the NBA to change some rules. And still, Chamberlain dominated basketball in ways the sport had never seen before or since.

Chamberlain was from Philadelphia, Pennsylvania. In high school, he received more than 200 scholarship offers from colleges around the country. He settled on Kansas. He could play both basketball and run track there. Chamberlain played

on Kansas' freshman basketball team in 1955–56. The NCAA did not allow freshmen to play on the varsity team at the time. He joined the varsity team in his sophomore season.

Chamberlain's career started with a bang. His first varsity game was against the Northwestern Wildcats. Chamberlain scored 52 points and pulled down 31 rebounds in the win. Through the 2010–11 season, the 52 points remained the single-game scoring record at Kansas. And Chamberlain did it in his first game!

Chamberlain was bigger and stronger than most of his opponents. He also was a skilled scorer and an excellent passer for his size. During his two seasons at Kansas, Chamberlain averaged 29.9 points and 18.3 rebounds per game. Through 2010–11, both numbers were still the highest in Jayhawks history.

Chamberlain led the Jayhawks to a 24–3 record in his first season. Then they advanced to the 1957 national championship game against the North Carolina Tar Heels. It took three overtimes to decide the winner. North Carolina came out on top, 54–53. Chamberlain was double- and triple-teamed throughout the contest. But he still had 23 points and 14 rebounds. Although the Jayhawks lost, Chamberlain was named the Most Outstanding Player of the tournament.

RULE CHANGES

Center Wilt Chamberlain was so good that the NCAA had to change some rules to slow him down. The NCAA widened the lane to keep Chamberlain from playing so close to the basket. It also changed inbounding rules and added an offensive goaltending rule because of Chamberlain. In addition, Chamberlain would take a running start on his free throws, leap toward the basket, and try to drop the ball into the hoop. So, the NCAA added a rule that said that a player must remain behind the free-throw line on a foul shot. The NBA also adopted many of these rule changes because of Chamberlain.

Chamberlain struggled with injuries during his junior season. However, he still averaged 30.1 points per game. That still stood as a Kansas record after the 2010–11 season. Chamberlain was also named an All-American for the second straight year. However, an 18–5 record was not good enough to get the Jayhawks into the NCAA Tournament.

ALLEN FIELDHOUSE

Starting in 1955, the Jayhawks began playing in Allen Fieldhouse. Sportswriter Mark Whicker once called it "the best place in America to watch college basketball." The fieldhouse is named after legendary Kansas coach Phog Allen. With a capacity of more than 16,000, Allen Fieldhouse is the largest basketball arena in Kansas.

Chamberlain decided to sign with the Harlem Globetrotters after his junior season. The Globetrotters are an exhibition team that tours the world. They play opponents while entertaining crowds with ball tricks, fancy shooting and dribbling, and off-the-wall routines. Chamberlain was not allowed to join the NBA at the time. A player could not join the NBA until his college class had graduated. But the Globetrotters gave him a chance to play professionally while getting a break from the triple-teaming defenses that frustrated him so much at Kansas.

Chamberlain played one year with the Globetrotters before joining the NBA. He spent 14 seasons there. Through 2010–11, no NBA player has averaged more rebounds per game than his 22.9. He also scored 100 points in one game in 1962. No other player has done that. Chamberlain was elected to the Naismith Basketball Hall of Fame in 1979.

The Jayhawks began to struggle after Chamberlain left. They finished just 11–15 in 1958–59. It was their first season with a losing record since 1947–48. The Jayhawks missed the postseason for five straight seasons from 1960–61 until 1964–65. In fact, it was not until 1971 that Kansas returned to the Final Four of the NCAA Tournament.

Kansas' Dave Nash attempts to block Louisville's Wes Unseld in a 1967 contest between the two teams.

Some of the best players at Kansas during the 1960s were forward Bill Bridges, center Walt Wesley, and guard Jo Jo White. Bridges played for the Jayhawks from 1958 to 1961. He was one of the greatest rebounders the school ever had. Wesley was an All-American in 1965 and 1966. White also was named an All-American twice, in 1968 and

1969. Kansas did reach the championship game of the National Invitation Tournament in 1968 but lost to Dayton.

The Jayhawks finally returned to the Final Four in 1971. The team finished 27–3 under head coach Ted Owens. Power forward Dave Robisch and shooting guard Isaac "Bud" Stallworth led the Jayhawks. Robisch was the main star in their first NCAA Tournament game that year. He recorded 29 points, 16 rebounds, six blocks, and four steals in that game. That helped Kansas beat the Houston Cougars 78–77. The Jayhawks then defeated the Drake Bulldogs to reach the Final Four.

However, they lost to the mighty UCLA Bruins 68–60. The Bruins went on to win their fifth of seven straight NCAA championships.

Kansas reached the Final Four one more time during the 1970s. Center Danny Knight and forwards Roger Morningstar and Norm Cook led the 1973–74 team. The Jayhawks' win over the Oral Roberts Titans in the Elite Eight was one of the most famous comebacks in Jayhawks history. They trailed the Titans by seven points with 2:40 remaining. Cook's late jumper sent the game into overtime. Forward Tommie Smith then scored two baskets in the final 44 seconds of overtime to help the Jayhawks win 93–90 and return to the Final Four. "It was the guttiest performance I've ever seen," Owens said.

Kansas went on to lose to Marquette in the Final Four. That left the Jayhawks without a national championship since 1952. But the next Kansas coach brought that drought to an end—in miraculous fashion.

ADOLPH RUPP

On December 10, 1977, Kansas played the Kentucky Wildcats at Allen Fieldhouse. As they played, legendary Kentucky coach Adolph Rupp passed away more than 600 miles (966 km) away in Lexington, Kentucky. He had been battling cancer and diabetes. Rupp had become famous as coach of Kentucky, where he guided the Wildcats from 1930 until 1972. However, Rupp actually got his start at Kansas. He played under Phog Allen from 1919 to 1923. The Jayhawks were awarded the Helms Athletic Foundation National Championship during Rupp's junior and senior seasons. As a coach, Rupp won four NCAA championships and notched a record 876 wins. The mark stood until 1997. Dean Smith, another Kansas graduate, surpassed it.

Kansas' Danny Manning looks to pass the ball around a Duke Blue Devils defender during the 1988 Final Four.

DANNY AND THE MIRACLES

KANSAS COACH TED OWENS WAS FIRED IN 1983. THE JAYHAWKS HAD JUST FINISHED BACK-TO-BACK LOSING SEASONS. LARRY BROWN REPLACED OWENS. HE LED THE TEAM FOR THE NEXT FIVE YEARS. THROUGH 2011, IT WAS THE SHORTEST STINT OF ANY COACH IN KANSAS BASKETBALL HISTORY. BUT IT WAS A PRODUCTIVE ONE.

The Jayhawks returned to the NCAA Tournament in Brown's first season, 1983–84. In fact, Kansas reached the NCAA Tournament in each of Brown's five seasons. The team had qualified for the tournament just once in the previous five seasons.

The 1983–84 team went 22–10 during the regular season. The Jayhawks were knocked out in the second round of the NCAA Tournament. But it was a step in the right direction.

A freshman forward named Danny Manning arrived on campus in the fall of 1984. The NCAA rule barring freshmen

DARNELL VALENTINE

Danny Manning was named a first-team All-American in 1985–86. It was the first time that a Kansas player had earned such an honor since Darnell Valentine in 1981. Valentine was a guard who was named first-team all-conference in each of his four seasons at Kansas. As of 2010–11, he is the school's all-time leader in free throws made (541) and steals (336). He was named the Jayhawks' Most Valuable Player in all four of his seasons there.

from the varsity team had been eliminated in 1972. So, Manning stepped right into the Kansas lineup. And he made an immediate impact. Manning averaged 14.6 points per game as a freshman. He was also named the Big Eight Conference's Newcomer of the Year. The Jayhawks went 26–8 that season and again reached the second round of the NCAA Tournament.

"I saw him play in high school," Brown said years later. "He was one of the finest young players I'd ever seen."

Kansas won 35 games during Manning's sophomore season. At the time, it was the most wins in school history. The team lost only four times. One of those defeats came against the Duke Blue Devils in the Final Four. The Jayhawks led the Blue Devils 65–61 with just over four minutes left. Manning fouled out late in the game, though. Duke rallied for the 71–67 win.

"I think if any team deserved to win a national championship, that team probably deserved it as much as any," Brown said.

Kansas posted a 25–11 record the following season. Manning increased his scoring average from 16.7 points to 23.9 points per game. His rebounds also increased by a large margin, from 6.3 to 9.5 per game. Manning was named a first-team All-American. But Kansas was unable to return to the Final Four of the NCAA Tournament. Instead, the Jayhawks were eliminated in the Sweet 16.

Manning had only one more season left at Kansas. He had only one more chance to lead the Jayhawks to their first NCAA championship in more than three decades. And the All-American forward did not disappoint.

In his senior season, Manning raised his scoring average to a career-high 24.8 points per game. He became the all-time leading scorer in

DANNY AND THE MIRACLES

[29]

In 1986, Kansas guard Kevin Pritchard, *left*, became the first player to make a three-point shot in Allen Fieldhouse.

Kansas history with 2,951 points. He also set the school record for career rebounds with 1,187. He was named a first-team All-American for the second straight season.

Manning had some help in the scoring department. Sophomore point guard Kevin Pritchard and junior swingman Milt Newton also played big roles. The team was talented and experienced. But the Jayhawks also experienced their share of problems during the season.

Kansas lost its first two games of the 1987–88 season against Iowa and Illinois. The Jayhawks also dropped five games in a row during the middle of the season. By the end of the regular season, the Jayhawks had 17 wins and 10 losses. They were considered a "bubble team" for the

NCAA Tournament. That meant they were not certain to be selected to play in the tournament.

Kansas defeated the Oklahoma State Cowboys before losing to the Kansas State Wildcats in the Big Eight Conference Tournament. Still, their 18–11 record was good enough to earn a number-six seed in the NCAA Tournament.

The Jayhawks opened the tournament with three victories to reach the Elite Eight. That meant a rematch against conference rival Kansas State for a berth in the Final Four. It was the fourth time Kansas and Kansas State had met that season. Kansas State had won two of the first three. But this matchup went the Jayhawks' way. Manning scored 20 points. And he had plenty of help. Newton scored 18 points and added nine rebounds and seven assists. Meanwhile, guard Scooter Barry scored a career-high 15 points off the bench.

The 71–58 victory set the stage for a Final Four showdown against Duke. The Blue Devils had eliminated the Jayhawks in the NCAA

TO THE PROS

The Los Angeles Clippers selected Danny Manning with the top pick in the 1988 NBA Draft. Manning played 15 seasons in the NBA with seven different teams. He made the All-Star team with the Clippers in 1993 and again in 1994. He also won the league's Sixth Man of the Year Award in 1998 while with the Phoenix Suns. In all, Manning averaged 14 points and 5.2 rebounds over 883 NBA games. In March 2007, he was named an assistant coach of the Kansas basketball team under Bill Self. In November 2008, Manning was elected to the National College Basketball Hall of Fame.

DANNY AND THE MIRACLES

Tournament's final weekend two years earlier. This time, Manning and company were ready for revenge.

Two years earlier, Manning had scored only four points in the loss against the Blue Devils. This time, he led the way with 25 points, 10 rebounds, and seven blocked shots. And this time, Kansas won, 66–59. Newton chipped in 20 points for Kansas. The Jayhawks advanced to face another familiar opponent in the national championship game.

The Oklahoma Sooners were one of Kansas' rivals in the Big Eight Conference. The Sooners entered the championship game with a 35–3 record. Kansas, meanwhile, was 27–10. The Sooners had scored more than 100 points 20 times. That included 152 points during one game in December. They had won 12 games by at least 30 points and had three players (guard Mookie Blaylock, forward Harvey Grant, and center Stacey King) who became top-12 picks in the NBA Draft.

Also, Oklahoma had beaten Kansas both times the teams had met that season. On paper, the national championship game looked like a mismatch. It turned out to be anything but.

The Jayhawks used two different types of offense to stick with the Sooners. In the first half, Kansas played a fast-paced style. The teams were tied 50–50 at halftime. In the second half, Kansas slowed things down. The Jayhawks led just 79–77 with 14 seconds left. That was when Manning took over. He made all four of his foul shots down the stretch to ice the victory.

The final score was Kansas 83, Oklahoma 79. The Jayhawks were national champions. Manning, who had 31 points and 18 rebounds in his final college game, was a March Madness legend.

"[Manning] wanted this one bad," King said afterward. "He went an extra level higher."

Newton made all six of his shots and finished with 15 points. Pritchard added 13 points on 6-for-7 shooting. The underdog Jayhawks, as a team, made 35 of 55 shots. They became the first team with 10 or more losses to win the NCAA championship.

"This team believed it could keep winning," Brown said. "We weren't afraid of anybody."

DANNY AND THE MIRACLES

Two-time All-American Raef LaFrentz of Kansas dunks the ball against the Connecticut Huskies in 1997.

THE MODERN JAYHAWKS

LARRY BROWN ACCEPTED A JOB COACHING WITH THE NBA'S SAN ANTONIO SPURS FOLLOWING KANSAS' 1988 NATIONAL CHAMPIONSHIP. IN NEED OF A NEW COACH, KANSAS TURNED TO NORTH CAROLINA TAR HEELS ASSISTANT COACH ROY WILLIAMS. HE HAD SPENT 10 SEASONS WITH THE TAR HEELS WORKING UNDER LEGENDARY COACH DEAN SMITH, A 1953 KANSAS GRADUATE. AS IT TURNED OUT, THE JAYHAWKS PICKED THE RIGHT MAN FOR THE JOB.

Williams guided Kansas to a 418–101 record during 15 seasons on the bench. No other Division I college basketball coach had ever won that many games in his first 15 seasons. Williams led the Jayhawks to four Final Fours and two trips to the NCAA Tournament title game. He was elected to the Naismith Basketball Hall of Fame in 2007.

Williams' first trip to the Final Four with the Jayhawks came in 1991. Forwards Mark Randall, Alonzo Jamison, and Mike Maddox led the team that season. The squad lost three

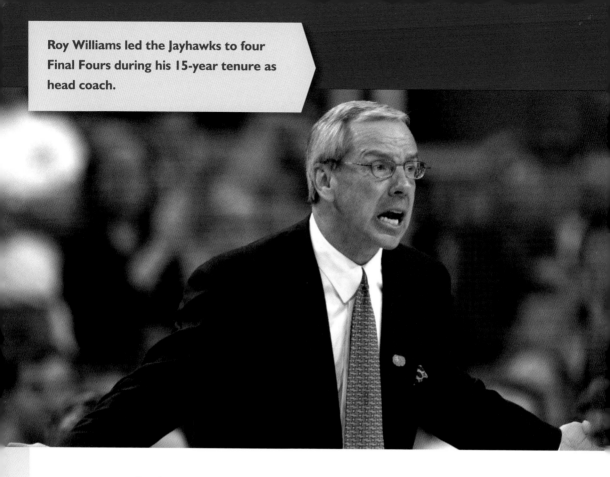

of its last six games heading into the NCAA Tournament. However, the Jayhawks recovered during the NCAA Tournament. They won five straight games, including upset victories against Indiana, Arkansas, and North Carolina. Kansas came up short in the national title game against another elite program. The Jayhawks fell to Duke, 72–65.

"It's a year we can really be proud of, and someday we'll be able to look back and see what we accomplished," Maddox said. "We came from nowhere and look where we ended up."

The Jayhawks advanced to the Final Four again two years later. A strong backcourt of point guard Adonis Jordan and shooting guard Rex Walters led the 1992–93 team. The Jayhawks won their first four games in the NCAA Tournament that year by an average of nearly 15 points per game. But North Carolina ended Kansas' season with a 78–68 victory in the Final Four.

From 1995 to 1998, the Jayhawks suffered through a stretch of NCAA Tournament disappointments. Kansas was a number-one seed in 1995, 1997, and 1998 and a number-two seed in 1996. But for four straight years, Kansas lost to a lower-seeded team in the tournament.

Those late 1990s teams featured some of the greatest players in Kansas history. Point guard Jacque Vaughn played from 1993–94 until 1996–97. He still had the second most assists in team history through 2010–11. Center Raef LaFrentz was named an All-American as both a junior and senior. He graduated in 1998 as the third-leading scorer in Jayhawks history. Small forward Paul Pierce was a 1998 first-team All-American. Through 2010–11 he still ranked among the Kansas leaders in many key categories despite only playing three years for the Jayhawks.

The early 2000s featured three more players who eventually had their jerseys retired at Kansas. All three arrived in Lawrence together in 1999.

RECORD WINS

Kansas set many school records during Roy Williams's first two seasons that still stood through the 2010–11 season. On January 3, 1989, the Jayhawks defeated Brown, 115–45. The 70-point victory remained the largest winning margin in school history. On December 9, 1989, Kansas set a school record for points in a game in a 150–95 romp against the Kentucky Wildcats. After that game, senior guard Kevin Pritchard said, "Outside of the NCAA Tournament, that's probably the most fun I've had here."

Kansas point guard Kirk Hinrich drives to the hoop during the 2002 NCAA Tournament.

They were point guard Kirk Hinrich and forwards Drew Gooden and Nick Collison. Together, they led the Jayhawks to the Final Four in 2002.

That year, Gooden averaged 19.8 points and 11.4 rebounds per game. Collison posted averages of 15.6 points and 8.3 rebounds. Hinrich averaged 14.8 points and five assists. Led by its three juniors,

Kansas became the first team in Big 12 Conference history to go undefeated in conference play. The top-seeded Jayhawks won their first four NCAA Tournament games. That included a 104–86 victory against Oregon to advance to the Final Four. It was their first Final Four appearance since 1993. However, a matchup with Maryland did not go Kansas' way in the Final Four. Just like that, the Jayhawks' season was over. So too was Gooden's college career. The All-American forward entered the NBA Draft after his junior season.

Even without Gooden, Kansas did not miss a beat during the 2002–03 season. Collison emerged as an All-American. Hinrich became one of the top guards in the country. Together, they led Kansas back to the Final Four. It was the school's first time reaching the Final Four in back-to-back seasons since 1952 and 1953.

Kansas faced Marquette and its star guard Dwyane Wade in the semifinal. That game turned out to be no contest. The Jayhawks rolled

AMONG THE GREATS

The 1996–97 Kansas Jayhawks did not win a national title. However, many consider that squad to be one of the best in school history. Led by future NBA players Paul Pierce, Raef LaFrentz, and Jacque Vaughn, the Jayhawks went 34–2 that season. They were ranked number one in the country for 15 straight weeks. They also won their conference tournament for the first time since 1992. The only two games the Jayhawks lost were a double-overtime thriller against the archrival Missouri Tigers in February and a heartbreaker against the Arizona Wildcats in the Sweet 16 of the NCAA Tournament. After the loss to Arizona, Vaughn said, "Sometimes, the best teams do not win."

to a 94–61 victory. Sophomore swingman Keith Langford led Kansas with 23 points. Collison had 12 points and 15 rebounds.

The championship game was a thriller between Kansas and Syracuse. The Jayhawks had two chances to tie the game in the final five seconds. But Kansas' Michael Lee had his three-pointer blocked. Then Hinrich shot an air ball at the buzzer, giving the Orangemen the championship.

Collison and Langford scored 19 points each. But the Jayhawks were doomed by their free-throw shooting. They made just 12 of 30 foul shots in a game they ended up losing by three points, 81–78.

One week later, Williams left Kansas to take over as head coach at his alma mater, North Carolina. "We are preparing for the next era of leadership in a heritage that goes back to James Naismith and Phog Allen," Kansas chancellor Robert Hemenway told Kansas players and recruits at the time. "KU has a long and successful men's basketball tradition and we want you to be part of that under our new head coach."

The Jayhawks found that and more under their next head coach. Bill Self was hired from the University of Illinois in 2003. He had an awful lot to live up to at Kansas. But after winning the 2008 NCAA Tournament— the first championship at Kansas since 1988—Self had earned his place in Jayhawks history.

It did not come easily. There were many NCAA Tournament disappointments under Williams. Several more Marches ended painfully under Self. But finally, on April 7, 2008, the Jayhawks were back on top of the college basketball world.

"[Coach Self] said, 'Believe, believe,'" recalled Mario Chalmers, the hero of the 2008 championship game. "We never gave up. We believed."

The Jayhawks continued to be one of the best teams in the nation. They were even ranked number one in the nation at times during the 2009–10 and 2010–11 seasons. However, NCAA Tournament disappointments continued. In the three seasons after their 2008 title, Kansas' best finish was a loss in the Elite Eight in 2011. Although NCAA Tournament success has not always come to Kansas, the school has an amazing tradition in basketball. In Lawrence, Kansas, the question is not *if* the Jayhawks will win another title, but *when* the Jayhawks' next title will be.

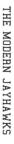

THE MODERN JAYHAWKS

TIMELINE

Dr. James Naismith, the inventor of the sport, becomes the first basketball coach at the University of Kansas.

Phog Allen takes over as Kansas coach and promptly leads the Jayhawks to their first Missouri Valley Conference title.

After posting a 16–2 record, Kansas is retroactively named national champions by the Helms Athletic Foundation.

Kansas is retroactively awarded the Helms Athletic Foundation national championship for a second straight season after going 17–1.

Fred Pralle becomes the first consensus All-American in Kansas basketball history.

1898   1907   1922   1923   1938

Kansas reaches the Final Four for a second straight season for the first time since 1952 and 1953. The Jayhawks make it to the national championship game before losing to the Syracuse Orangemen 81–78.

The Jayhawks win their first 21 games and 33 of their first 34 games before losing to the Arizona Wildcats in the Sweet 16 of the NCAA Tournament.

Kansas reaches the Final Four for the first of four times under coach Roy Williams. The Jayhawks lose to Duke 72–65 in the NCAA title game.

Danny Manning leads a Kansas team known as "Danny and the Miracles" to the NCAA Tournament title.

Kansas reaches the Final Four but loses to North Carolina in the national semifinals.

1988   1991   1993   1997   2003

Kansas, led by consensus first-team All-Americans Charlie B. Black and Ray Evans, wins its fourth straight Big Six Conference championship.

Kansas wins its first NCAA Tournament, defeating St. John's 80—63 in the championship game. All-American center Clyde Lovellette is named the Most Outstanding Player of the Final Four.

Wilt Chamberlain's first season for the Jayhawks ends with a triple-overtime loss to the North Carolina Tar Heels in the national championship game.

Chamberlain leaves Kansas after his junior season to sign with the Harlem Globetrotters.

Led by Dave Robisch and Bud Stallworth, Kansas reaches the Final Four for the first time in 14 years. The Jayhawks lose to UCLA in the national semifinals.

1943   1952   1957   1958   1971

The Jayhawks finish 23—7 but get upset by the Bucknell Bison in the first round of the NCAA Tournament. One year later, the Bradley Braves upset the Jayhawks in the first round of the NCAA Tournament.

Bill Self takes over as the Jayhawks' head coach after Roy Williams leaves to coach North Carolina.

For the first time since 1956—57, Kansas is selected as the number-one team in the Associated Press preseason poll prior to the 2004—05 season.

Kansas captures the NCAA Tournament championship for the third time in school history with a win over the Memphis Tigers.

Kansas defeats the Texas Tech Red Raiders 80—68 on March 11 for the 2,000th win in school history.

2003   2004   2005   2008   2010

QUICK STATS

PROGRAM INFO

University of Kansas
Jayhawks (1898–)

NCAA TOURNAMENT FINALS
(WINS IN BOLD)

1940, **1952**, 1953, 1957, **1988**, 1991, 2003, **2008**

OTHER ACHIEVEMENTS

Final Fours: 13
NCAA Tournaments: 40
Big 12 Tournament titles: 8

KEY PLAYERS
(POSITION(S); YEARS WITH TEAM)

Charlie B. Black (F; 1941–43; 1945–47)
Charlie T. Black (G; 1921–24)
Mario Chalmers (G; 2005–08)
Wilt Chamberlain (C; 1956–58)
Nick Collison (F; 1999–2003)
Paul Endacott (G; 1920–23)
Drew Gooden (F; 1999–2002)
Kirk Hinrich (G; 1999–2003)
Raef LaFrentz (F; 1994–98)
Clyde Lovellette (C; 1949–52)

Danny Manning (F; 1984–88)
Paul Pierce (F; 1995–98)
Darnell Valentine (G; 1977–81)
Jacque Vaughn (G; 1993–97)
Jo Jo White (G; 1965–69)

KEY COACHES

Forrest "Phog" Allen (1907–09; 1919–56):
    590–219; 10–3 (NCAA Tournament)
Larry Brown (1983–88):
    135–44; 14–4 (NCAA Tournament)
Bill Self (2003–):
    237–46; 16–7 (NCAA Tournament)
Roy Williams (1988–2003):
    418–101; 34–14 (NCAA Tournament)

HOME ARENA

Allen Fieldhouse (1955–)

* All statistics through 2010–11 season

QUOTES & ANECDOTES

"There can be no doubt—Kansas is college basketball. The game's inventor, Dr. James Naismith, was the Jayhawks' first coach. His pupil, Phog Allen, coached both Adolph Rupp and Dean Smith. And the players? From Wilt the Stilt [Chamberlain] to Danny [Manning] and the Miracles to Paul Pierce, KU has been the heartland's best program for more than 100 years." —*ESPN College Basketball Encyclopedia*

Wilt Chamberlain briefly hosted his own radio show, called "Flippin' with The Dipper," while he was at Kansas. Chamberlain used to play his favorite records, which were mostly jazz and blues. Chamberlain was following in the footsteps of Clyde Lovellette, who also had his own radio show at the same radio station. Lovellette played mostly country music, however.

"You don't coach basketball, Forrest, you play it." —Dr. James Naismith to Forrest "Phog" Allen, who became known as the "Father of Basketball Coaching"

The most popular chant among fans at Kansas basketball games is "Rock chalk, Jayhawk, KU." It began as "Rah rah, Jayhawk, KU," developed by Kansas chemistry professor E. H. S. Bailey in 1886. It was later changed to "Rock chalk" in reference to chalk rock, the name of the limestone found on Mount Oread on the Lawrence campus.

GLOSSARY

All-American
A group of players chosen as the best amateurs in the country in a particular activity.

alma mater
The school that someone attended.

alumnus
A graduate of a school.

backcourt
The point guards and shooting guards on a basketball team.

conference
In sports, a group of teams that plays each other each season.

consensus
Unanimous agreement.

draft
A system used by professional sports leagues to select new players in order to spread incoming talent among all teams. The NBA Draft is held each June.

eligibility
The quality of having the right to do something, satisfying the appropriate conditions.

legend
An extremely famous person, especially in a particular field.

recruit
To secure the services of a player to join a college basketball team.

rivals
Opponents that bring out great emotion in a team, its fans, and its players.

scholarship
Financial assistance awarded to students to help them pay for school. Top athletes earn scholarships to represent a college through its sports teams.

seed
In basketball, a ranking system used for tournaments. The best teams earn a number-one seed.

upset
A result where the supposedly worse team defeats the supposedly better team.

varsity
The main team that represents a school.

FOR MORE INFORMATION

FURTHER READING

Davis, Ken. *The University of Kansas Basketball Vault*. Atlanta, GA: Whitman Publishing, 2008.

Editors of ESPN. *ESPN College Basketball Encyclopedia: The Complete History of the Men's Game*. New York: Ballantine Books and ESPN Books, 2009.

Fulks, Matt. *Echoes of Kansas Basketball: The Greatest Stories Ever Told*. Chicago, IL: Triumph Books, 2006.

WEB LINKS

To learn more about the Kansas Jayhawks, visit ABDO Publishing Company online at **www.abdopublishing.com.** Web sites about the Jayhawks are featured on our Book Links page. These links are routinely monitored and updated to provide the most current information available.

PLACES TO VISIT

Allen Fieldhouse
1651 Naismith Drive
Lawrence, KS 66045
785-864-3141
www.kuathletics.com/facilities/kan-allen-fieldhouse.html

This has been the Jayhawks' arena since 1955. It is named after Forrest "Phog" Allen, the legendary Kansas coach who guided the team for 39 seasons between 1907 and 1956. Tours are available when the Jayhawks are not playing.

Kansas Sports Museum
Newton Chisholm Trail Center
601 SE 36th - Suite 123
Newton, KS 67114
316-804-4686
www.kshof.org

This Hall of Fame and museum depicts some of the greatest players, coaches and moments in the history of Kansas sports. The museum includes exhibits dating back to James Naismith and Phog Allen, as well as more modern exhibits about great players such as Wilt Chamberlain, Danny Manning, and Paul Pierce. Guided tours are available.

INDEX

ABOUT THE AUTHOR

Drew Silverman is a sportswriter based in Philadelphia, Pennsylvania. He graduated from Syracuse University in 2004. He then worked as a sportswriter and editor at ESPN's headquarters in Bristol, Connecticut, before returning back home to Philadelphia. After several years as the sports editor for *The Bulletin* newspaper, he began working for Comcast SportsNet as an editorial content manager. He has covered everything from college basketball to the Stanley Cup Finals.